World Cuisine | **Japan**

Japan

With dishes by:

Hiromitsu Nozaki • Seiji Yamamoto

World Cuisine

WORLD CUISINE - Japan

Coordination: ESP Promotions Ltd, London
And TP& Associates, Madrid and Milan

For further information on the collection or to purchase
any books that you have missed, please visit:
www.timesonline.co.uk/cookbooks

For further information regarding publication rights,
please contact: cookbookinfo@gmail.com

© Ciro Ediciones, S.A., Barcelone

Original idea
Jaume Fàbregas

Editorial director
Juan Manuel Bellver

Collection coordinator
Núria Egido

Culinary advisors
Xavier Agulló
R. de Nola
Jorge Osés

Editors
Mercè Bolló
Pau Raya Castell
Miguel Ángel Sánchez

Contributing editors
Esther Buira
Lola Hernández
M.ª Dolores Escudero
David Ibáñez
Carles Llurda
Meritxell Piqué
Carles Raventós
Mihoko Sugita

Photography
Daniel Loewe / Joan Jolis, S.L.

Layout
New Color Book, S.L.

Cover design
WEP Milano

Preprint
Digitalscreen

Printers
Avenida Gráfica

ISBN 84-609-7351-4 (complete works)
ISBN 84-609-7359-X (volume VI – JAPAN)
Legal deposit: M-39748-2005

© of photographs, introduction and drinks: Stock Photos

Contents

World Cuisine: Japan

Japanese cuisine is pleasing to the eye and tempting for the palate. Its unquestionable influence on the most innovative gastronomies is due to its long standing relationship with other oriental cultures, the influence of Buddhism and the international isolation that it experienced for centuries.

For all these reasons, this cuisine is a pleasure that must be treated with respect and without prejudice.

When looking at Japanese cuisine for the first time, you feel a curious mixture of admiration and apprehension: admiration due to its delicate and colourful presentation, yet a sense of apprehension due to its use of raw or hardly cooked foods. Little by little, Japanese cooking has managed to overcome this initial obstacle and since the start of the 21st century has achieved a prestigious place amongst the most influential gastronomies in the world. The most important breakthrough between European and Japanese cuisine was in the 1970's, when *nouvelle cuisine* was inspired by the attractive presentation employed in Japanese dishes. It was an insight into this little known cuisine, that over time has been able to merge foreign influences with traditional local recipes, creating a whole new set of individual dishes. One of the best kept trademarks of Japanese cuisine is simplicity, with the aim of keeping the natural taste of products and using a limited amount of basic ingredients.

The country of rice

As with the majority of oriental cooking, rice plays a major role in Japanese cuisine. It is an essential element in all meals. Rice is also important in *sushi*, a stereotypical Japanese dish of which countless varieties exist. The most used fish and seafood in *sushi* are tuna, sea bass or king prawns, due to their mild taste and colouring. Another way of preparing raw fish is called *sashimi*, which is again fillets of raw fish or seafood but this time without the rice.

Both specialities are served with soy sauce and a spicy paste called *wasabi*. Another fundamental ingredient is soya, from which *tofu, miso* and other sauces are obtained – these are the basic flavourings used in Japanese dishes. Other key ingredients in Japanese cuisine includes various types of fish, seafood, algae, fresh vegetables, noodles and aromatic herbs and spices all combined to create a varied, simple yet balanced diet.

The limited presence of meat is due to the shortage of land that made it difficult to keep animals, as well as the influence of Buddhism

that was introduced from China in the 6th century. This resulted in the adoption of vegetarian habits, given that the slaughtering and consumption of animals is condemned by Buddhism. Contact with neighbouring China, also brought about the introduction of tea, soya and the trademark chopsticks. However, there are also notable differences between Chinese and Japanese gastronomy, for example cooking methods: Chinese cooking fries food quickly, while Japanese hardly use oil. Food is roasted directly over a heat or on a grill, or cooked in a little water or steamed. One of the defining moments in the history of Japanese culture was the development of Zen Buddhism that promoted the ritual tea ceremony. Despite contact with other oriental cultures, the country's history has been mainly characterised by international isolation, only broken in the 16th century with the arrival of Portuguese expeditions, which introduced food covered in batter, origin of the popular *tempura*.

At the end of the 19th century, Japan opened up properly to the world when they started to trade and adopt new cooking techniques. Currently, Japanese food is found in the *kaiseki (traditional)* restaurants, small places specialising in *sushi* or *tempura* or in the numerous street stalls. The busy lives of students and workers have also created a "take away" culture which has its own individual style – the *bento,* that includes simple dishes, like rice, meat or roasted fish and vegetables. Lastly, it is worth mentioning the special ceremonies that take place in the *kaiseki* restaurants, whose cuisine is considered to be of the highest order, with legions of dishes of different colours and textures. In general, the menu at the *kaiseki* restaurants is made up of a soup, starters, salads, boiled and roasted dishes, sautéed vegetables and of course rice. Despite the apparent excess, the lightness of Japanese meals enables food to be digested easily. Now you have to discover, recipe by recipe, some of its cooking secrets – a real delight for the senses.

World Cuisine

Starters

This collection of traditional dishes
has been created by:

Takashi Kamura
Restaurant Bun Sichi

Hideki Matsuhisa
Restaurant Shunka

Takashi Ochiai
Ochiai Bakery

Level of difficulty: medium
Preparation time: 40 minutes
Cooking time: 15 minutes

Misoshiru
Miso and *tofu* soup

Serves 4 people
3 tablespoons miso
2 tablespoons of wakame
(a silky textured seaweed
available from oriental stores)
125g firm tofu
1 spring onion
500ml dashi *stock*

First, make the *dashi* stock. For this, use 10g of *kombu* (dried giant seaweed) and 15g of dry tuna (*hana-katsuo* or bonito flakes) per 500ml of water. Clean the *kombu* with a damp cloth and leave to soak in water in a saucepan for 30 minutes. Cook in the same water over a moderate heat for about 10 minutes. Remove the *wakame* and add half of the tuna. Bring the stock to boil, remove from the heat and leave to rest until the tuna flakes have descended to the bottom of the pan and drain.

Put the *wakame* in a bowl with water and leave to soak for about 15 minutes, until it completely opens. Drain and chop if necessary.

Cut the spring onion in thin slices and cut the *tofu* into small cubes. Put the *miso* into a pan and mix with a little of the stock. Heat the rest of the stock over a low heat and add the dissolved *miso*, *wakame* and *tofu*. Without boiling, finally add the fine slices of spring onion and immediately remove from the heat and serve hot.

In Japan, the quality of stock is judged by its transparency and aromatic richness.

Level of difficulty: low
Preparation time: 15 minutes
Cooking time: 15 minutes

Chawanmushi
Curdled egg soup

Serves 4 people
4-6 eggs
500ml dashi *stock*
1 tablespoon sake
1/2 teaspoon salt
1/2 tablespoon soy sauce
4-8 king prawns
4 shitake mushrooms
Assorted white fish
Assorted vegetables

First make the *dashi* stock (see *Misoshiru,* previous recipe page 12). Lightly beat the eggs in a bowl and add the *dashi* stock, *sake*, salt and soy sauce. Slowly stir the mixture until the salt has dissolved; avoid making a mousse. Filter the mixture through a fine cotton cloth or folded gauze and divide into four individual bowls. Cut the fish, thinly slice the vegetables and divide between the four bowls. Add one or two peeled king prawns to each dish. Cover the bowls with aluminium foil and steam the soup or cook in a bowl set over simmering water for 15 minutes, until the egg starts to curdle. Remove from heat and leave to stand for a while for the egg to finish curdling. Serve hot.

Although this dish is presented in the soup category, when the egg curdles it forms a creamy rather than soup-like texture.

Ika to kyuri to wakame no sunomono
Squid, cucumber and *wakame* in a vinaigrette dressing

Level of difficulty: low
Preparation time: 20 minutes

Serves 4 people
2 cucumbers
2 wakame *leaves*
4 medium sized squids (without tentacles)
Salt

For the *amazu* vinaigrette:
1/2 cup rice vinegar
1/2 teaspoon soy sauce
1 tablespoon sugar

Peel the cucumber, cut into very fine slices and then cut in half. If preferred, you can remove the middle part of the cucumber before cutting into slices. Add salt and leave to stand for about 15 minutes in a colander. Leave the *wakame* to soak for 15 minutes, until it has completely opened and drain. Cut the squids into strips and blanch until they are soft.

Make the vinaigrette with the rice vinegar, soy sauce and sugar. Divide into four bowls and add the half slices of cucumber, the *wakame* and squid.

In Japan, *Sunomono* is the equivalent to our salads. It has a very refreshing taste and increases the appetite.

Tempura udon
Noodle soup with king prawn tempura

Level of difficulty: medium
Preparation time: 30 minutes
Cooking time: 15 minutes

Serves 4 people
240g udon *noodles*
6 small cups dashi *stock (500ml)*
1 spring onion
1 small cup soy sauce
1 small cup of rice wine

For the *tempura*:
8 king prawns
2 cups of fine white rice flower
1 1/2 cups of ice water

Prepare the stock by mixing six small cups of *dashi* stock with a small cup of soy sauce and rice wine. Keep hot.

Boil the noodles in plenty of water for 10-15 minutes, drain and add to the stock.

Cut the spring onion in fine slices and scatter over the stock.

Prepare the batter (*tempura*) by mixing the rice flower with the iced water. Gently mix the batter together to avoid lumps.

Peel the prawns, leaving the end of the tail in place. Remove the intestines and make small cuts along the abdomen to avoid them from shrinking when frying. Coat the prawns in the batter and fry in very hot oil.

Serve on top of the noodles.

The oil must be at a very high temperature, about 180°C, so that the batter goes very crispy.

Yakisoba
Sautéed noodles
with squid and king prawns

Level of difficulty: medium
Preparation time: 20 minutes
Cooking time: 30 minutes

Serves 4 people
200g soba noodles
1 small cup yakisoba sauce
12 king prawns
100g squid
30g Chinese leaves
30g carrots
30g onion
Dried tuna flakes (katsuobushi)

Boil the noodles in plenty of water until *al dente*, wash them in cold water and leave to one side, adding a little oil so that they do not stick together. Chop the squid and sauté together with the peeled king prawns and a little salt and pepper. When they are half-cooked, add the Chinese leaves, carrots and sliced onion to the frying pan. Once they are cooked, add the noodles and small cup of *yakisoba* and sauté together with the rest of the ingredients. Decorate the dish with some flakes of dried tuna.

Many dishes in day-to-day Japanese cooking are influenced by Chinese cuisine, and this is one of the most popular ones.

Zarusoba
Noodles served on a wooden mat

Level of difficulty: medium
Preparation time: 30 minutes
Cooking time: 15 minutes

Serves 4 people
400g soba noodles
1 sheet of nori seaweed
3-4 teaspoons wasabi (paste or powder)
2 spring onions (green part)

For the sauce:
400ml water
80ml soy sauce
80ml mirin (rice wine)
20ml dashi stock

Cook the *soba* noodles in plenty of water for eight minutes. When they are cooked, drain them and wash in cold water. Roast the sheet of *nori* algae (the rough part) over a low heat and cut into irregular pieces if cutting by hand or regular and sliced pieces if cutting with scissors. If the *wasabi* is in powder form, prepare the paste by mixing an equal quantity of powder and water.

To make the sauce, mix all the ingredients together in a pan and cook over a medium heat until the *mirin* alcohol evaporates. When it cools, put it in the fridge. The noodles are to be placed on a wooden mat over a plate and scatter the pieces of *nori* algae over the top. The sauce, *wasabi* and soft spring onion are served separately as side dishes. The diners prepare the sauce according to their tastes and dip the noodles in it before eating.

It is important that the sauce is very cold at the time of serving, as this is a refreshing summer dish.

Hiyayakko
Cold *tofu*

Serves 4 people
400g tofu
Dried tuna flakes
*(*katsuobushi*)*
2 spring onions
Soy sauce

Cut the fresh *tofu* in cubes and divide onto individual plates. Decorate with a spring onion cut into very fine slices and some dried tuna flakes (*katsuobushi*). Serve with soy sauce that can be poured over the *tofu* or served apart in individual bowls.

In the past, there were Japanese specialists that, like Western bakers, got up especially early to prepare fresh *tofu* each day.

Level of difficulty: medium
Preparation time: 10 minutes
Cooking time: 10 minutes

Tofu teriyaki
Tofu with teriyaki sauce

Serves 4 people
8 tofu *cubes*
4 *garlic cloves*
Corn flour

For the teriyaki sauce:
1 small cup soy sauce
1 tablespoon mirin
2 tablespoons sugar

Cover the cubes of *tofu* with the corn flour, fry in very hot oil until they are golden brown and put to one side on absorbent paper. Cut the garlic cloves lengthways, fry and keep to one side. To prepare the *teriyaki* sauce, mix the soy sauce, sugar and *mirin* together and fry over a medium heat. When the sauce is hot, add the cubes of *tofu* and fried garlic to the frying pan.

The amount of ingredients for the *teriyaki* sauce can vary according to taste. A little *sake* can be added as well if required (see *Gyu no kushiyaki*).

Namasu sarada
Daikon radish and carrot salad (*mooli*)

Level of difficulty: low
Preparation time: 20 minutes

Serves 4 people

250g daikon *radish (also known as* mooli*)*
2 medium sized carrots
1 teaspoon black sesame seeds
1 small cup rice vinegar
Salt

Finely grate the *daikon* radish and carrots and separate them in two bowls. Cover with very cold water and leave to soak for about 15-20 minutes. Drain well, add salt, stir and separate into portions. Individually serve the salad in a dome shape. Decorate with black sesame seeds, lemon grind or very fine strips of lime. Pour the rice vinegar over the salad or serve separately.

A refreshing salad which is ideally served with meat and fish dishes.

Level of difficulty: low
Preparation time: 2 hours
30 minutes

Shimesaba sarada
Mackerel salad

Serves 4 people
150g mackerel fillet
Sea salt
Rice vinegar
Mixture of lettuces
4 chicory leaves
Wakame *(a silky textured seaweed)*
Kombu *(kelp seaweed)*

Clean the mackerel fillets making sure all of the bones are removed. Cover with sea salt and leave to marinate for two hours. Remove the salt and clean the mackerel with a cloth that has been soaked in rice vinegar. Then, leave the mackerel to soak for twenty minutes in a container full of rice vinegar. Place the fillets on absorbent kitchen roll and cut into fine strips. Place on the plate on top of a bed of lettuce leaves, julienne strips of chicory leaves, and the *wakame* and *kombu*.

This dish is typically eaten in Autumn.

Level of difficulty: low
Preparation time: 20 minutes
Cooking time: 5 minutes

Kimpira
Sautéed green beans

Serves 4 people
250g green beans (or salsifis)
2 tablespoons vegetable oil
2 tablespoons sake
2 tablespoons soy sauce
1 tablespoon sugar
1 chilli

Wash the green beans and cut into very fine strips.

Cut open the chilli, remove the seeds and then chop.

Place a frying pan over the heat with oil and add the green beans and chopped chilli. Sauté for two or three minutes until the green beans start to soften.

Then, add the *sake*, soy sauce and sugar to the pan. Lower the heat to avoid burning the sugar. Continue sautéing the green beans until practically all the liquid has evaporated.

Kimpira is the name in Japanese for sautéed fine green bean strips. Out of all the recipes, the most typical is the kimpira gobo, with burdock root.

Level of difficulty: low
Preparation time: 15 minutes
Cooking time: 10 minutes

Yakitori
Chicken skewers

Serves 4 people
4 chicken thighs
2 spring onions
Salt
Pepper

Cut the skinless, clean chicken into cubes, and the spring onion in pieces of about 2 centimetres long. Place alternating chicken cubes and spring onion pieces onto the bamboo skewers.

For the *yakitori* sauce:
4 tablespoons soy sauce
2 tablespoons sake
2 tablespoons mirin
1 tablespoon thick soy sauce (tamari)
1 tablespoon sugar

To make the sauce, mix all the ingredients in a pan and bring to boil over a slow heat until a third of the sauce has evaporated. Season the chicken skewers and roast them over charcoal, or on a grill, dipping them two or three times in the *yakitori* sauce during cooking. Serve hot with the remaining sauce in a separate dish.

In Japan, *yakitori* is more often seen in a bar or restaurant than in the family home, although it is one of the most popular and well-known Japanese aperitifs.

Level of difficulty: medium
Preparation time: 1 hour
30 minutes
Cooking time: 10 minutes

Gyoza
Small Japanese dumplings

Serves 4 people
(16 dumplings)

For the puff pastry:
100g flour
85ml water

For the filling:
150g minced pork
120g Chinese leaves
2 spring onions
2 soft garlics
30g ginger
6 tablespoons sake
4 tablespoons soy sauce
2 tablespoons sesame oil
Salt and pepper

For the sauce:
1/2 small cup soy sauce
1/2 cup rice vinegar
2 tablespoons water
1 teaspoon sesame oil
1/2 teaspoon shichimi *or seven spice powder (it is widely available in oriental stores)*

Mix the water with the flour to make a consistent and homogeneous paste. Cover with a damp cloth and leave to stand for about 15 minutes. Once this time has passed, cut pieces of pastry into disc shapes of around 10 centimetres in diameter (alternatively you can buy gyozo skins in Chinese and Japanese stores and use these).

Finely chop the Chinese leaves, garlic and ginger and leave in a container mixed with the minced pork. Pour the *sake*, sesame oil and soy sauce into the container, add salt and pepper and leave to stand (without being cooked) for an hour. Place a tablespoon of filling in the centre of the disc, fold them in half and seal them with water at the edges. Fill a pan with water and when it starts to boil, add the parcels. Cover the pan and place over a slow heat for two or three minutes. To finish, drain the water that has not evaporated and fry the parcels with a little oil until golden brown. For the accompanying sauce, add all the ingredients and mix.

Gyoza is not a main dish; it is more usually eaten as a starter or side dish.

Level of difficulty: low
Preparation time: 15 minutes
Cooking time: 60 minutes

Anko no kimo
Monkfish liver

Serves 4 people
*300g monkfish liver (anko-
Japanese version of foie-gras)*
1 small cup sake
1 spring onion
Daikon *(a mild white radish also
known as* mooli*)*

For the *ponzu* sauce:
50cl soy sauce
*50cl citric juice (yuzu, lemon,
lime, etc.)*

Remove the sinews and fat from the liver and clean well. Then, cut into thick strips and soak in the *sake*. Wrap the strips in aluminium foil and steam cook for one hour. Leave to cool and cut into small portions.

The monkfish liver is served with chopped spring onion, grated *daikon* radish and *ponzu* sauce. This sauce is made by mixing the soy sauce together with the juice of any citric fruit, or can be bought from a specialist shop.

Monkfish liver, known as *foie* from the sea, is highly valued and expensive in Japan. It has a strong taste and a very oily texture.

Level of difficulty: medium
Preparation time: 30 minutes
Cooking time: 5-10 minutes

Kakiage
Mixed *tempura*

Serves 4 people
2 medium sized cuttlefish
1 onion
2 carrots
1 courgette
1 green pepper
2 tablespoons wheat flour

For the *tentsuyu* sauce:
*1 small cup dashi stock (see
page 14 Misoshiro)*
1/2 small cup of rice wine
1/2 small cup soy sauce
Grated daikon radish (mooli)
Grated ginger

For the *tempura* batter:
2 cups of fine white rice flower
1 1/2 cups ice water
*gently mix together to avoid
lumps*

Clean the cuttlefish, cut into strips and leave in a bowl.

Slice the vegetables finely and add to the bowl with the strips of cuttlefish, together with 2 tablespoons of wheat flour, this absorbs the liquid and helps stick the batter to the vegetables. Put a deep frying pan with plenty of oil (5-6cm) over a high heat until it reaches about 180°C. Meanwhile, prepare the batter. Empty the batter over the ingredients and stir to mix everything together. When the oil reaches the correct temperature start frying the mixture in small batches so that the batter turns golden brown. Drain on kitchen roll to remove oil.

Prepare the *tentsuyu* sauce by heating the *dashi* stock, rice wine and soy sauce in a pan and bring to the boil.

When it starts to boil, remove from the heat and serve hot with the grated *daikon* (*mooli*) and ginger.

The Spanish and Portuguese missionaries who arrived in the 16th century introduced this method of battering food into Japan. It is possible that it was related to Lent, given that a meat tempura does not exist.

Level of difficulty: low
Preparation time: 2 hours
Cooking time: 5 minutes

Asari no sakamushi
Sake clams

Serves 4 people
500g clams
1/2 small cup sake
1/2 teaspoon salt
2 spring onions

Wash the clams well and leave to stand in salted water for a couple of hours to wash away all the sand.

Finely chop the spring onions. Empty the *sake* into a saucepan and place over a high heat. Add salt. When it starts to boil, add the clams then immediately cover and leave to cook for about three minutes, stirring the pan a couple of times. Once the clams open, turn off the heat and add the spring onions. Cover again for two more minutes.

Sake brings a special aroma and taste to this recipe.

World Cuisine

Main courses

Level of difficulty: high
Preparation time: 60 minutes
Rice cooking time: 30 minutes

Maki zushi
Sushi

Serves 4 people

*3 cups rice (500g) for Japanese
sushi (or Calasparra rice)*
2 cups water (600ml)
10 x 10cm kombu *(kelp
seaweed sold dried)*
3 tablespoons sake
4 sheets nori *seaweed*
Tuna
*Salmon (must be extremely fresh
cut into thin strips, cover and
chill until needed)*

For the *awasezu* vinaigrette:
1/2 cup rice vinegar
3 tablespoons sugar
2 teaspoons salt

Prepare the rice for the *sushi*. Clean the *kombu* with a damp cloth and leave in a container with 3 cups of water for 30 minutes. Add to a pan the water from the *kombu* , *sake* and cleaned, drained rice. Cover. When boiled, take out the *kombu*, re-cover and leave the rice to boil for 10-15 minutes over a slow heat. Meanwhile, prepare the vinaigrette by mixing the three ingredients together in a pan over a high heat until it starts to boil. Switch off the heat and leave the vinaigrette to cool. Spread the rice out in a round wooden container called *handai* or in a bowl. While hot, pour into the vinaigrette and stir with great care so that the rice soaks up the vinaigrette without the grains being broken. At the same time, use a fan to cool it, so that the remaining liquid evaporates and gives a better presentation and taste. Leave the rice covered with a damp cloth so that it does not dry, until completely cooled.

To make the *maki* rolls, lay the bamboo mat or grease proof paper out over a flat surface and place the toasted *nori* sheet on top (with the shiny side facing down).

Add 2-3 tablespoons of rice to the centre and spread over the *nori*, leaving 1.5 cm margin at the sides, until a fine,

Continued on next page

uniformed layer is created. Place the filling ingredients (tuna or salmon) onto the centre forming a horizontal strip. Lift the edge of the mat and roll it from one side to the other, holding the ingredients in place with the fingers. Unroll the mat to obtain a cylinder shape of *sushi*. Roll the cylinder a few times so that the *sushi* stays firm. Cut the cylinder in 3cm pieces with a wet knife, to avoid the rice sticking to it.

Sushi is a stereotypical dish in Japanese cooking and is the most popular in the West, although not everyone knows the different varieties, such as *maki, nigiri* and *temaki*.

Level of difficulty: medium
Preparation time: 40 minutes
Rice cooking time: 30 minutes

Temaki zushi
Seaweed and rice cones

Serves 4 people
200g rice prepared for sushi
10 sheets nori *seaweed*
1 Japanese omelette
1/2 cucumber sliced
8 king prawns
4 shitake mushrooms
*Marinated pumpkin (*kampyo*)*
Marinated daikon *radish*
*(*takuwan*)*
Soy sauce
Wasabi

Prepare the rice for the *sushi*. (see *Maki zushi*, page 46). Cook the king prawns in water with salt, then peel them. Cut the cucumber into slices. Clean, chop and sauté the *shitake* mushrooms. Wash the marinated pumkin and marinated *daikon* slices. Cut the *nori* seaweed sheets into four equal parts with scissors. Prepare a Japanese omelette (*tomagoyaki*) and cut into strips.

To make a Japanese omelette, you need 4 eggs, 1 teaspoon of sugar, 3 teaspoons of *sake*, 2 teaspoons of soy sauce and half a tablespoon of oil.

Beat the eggs and add the *sake*, soy sauce and sugar. Keep beating until the sugar has dissolved. Over a high heat, add a little oil to a frying pan. Put in a quarter of the egg mixture and spread. When it has half curdled, roll it from the other end of the pan towards you. Add a little more oil and move the omelette to the back of the pan. Empty another quarter of the egg mixture into the pan and spread evenly, lifting the first omelette up so the egg starts to curdle underneath. Roll the second omelette on top of the first and repeat the process until you have four rolled omelettes.

Continued on next page

To make the cones, take a rectangle of *nori* seaweed with your hand. Spread the rice out on top and add the mixture of chosen ingredients. Then, roll the algae in a cone shape. Soy sauce and *wasabi* are served with this *temaki* dish.

The "Te" from *temaki* means hands and "*maki*" means to roll. Therefore *temaki zushi* is a *sushi* roll made with the hands. It is perhaps the easiest to make.

Level of difficulty: high
Preparation time: 50 minutes
Rice cooking time: 30 minutes

Nigiri zushi
Nigiri sushi balls

Serves 4 people
(40 pieces)
800g rice prepared for sushi
Salmon roe
Mackerel
Eel
Red tuna
Oily tuna
Salmon
King prawns
Wasabi

Prepare the rice for the *sushi.* (see *Maki zushi*, page 46). Wet your hands to avoid the rice sticking to you. Take a handful of rice in your right hand and form a round shape. Keep the ball of rice in your right hand and put in the palm of your left hand one of the raw fish fillets (or a blanched king prawn, opened at the abdomen, braised eel or another chosen ingredient) Spread with *wasabi*. Place the ball of rice on top of the fish with the *wasabi* and exert a light pressure so that they merge. Serve the other way round with the fish on top.

Nigiri zushi is typical of the Kanto region, although it is eaten in all of Japan.

Level of difficulty: medium
Preparation time: 50 minutes
Cooking time: 25 minutes

Sanshoku soboro don
Tricolour *domburi*

Serves 4 people
4 cups white rice
20 green beans
Salt

For the scrambled eggs:
4 eggs
1 tablespoon mirin *(rice wine)*
1 teaspoon sugar
Salt

For the chicken:
200g diced chicken
4 tablespoons soy sauce
2 tablespoons sake
1 tablespoon mirin
1 tablespoon ginger juice
1 teaspoon sugar

Firstly prepare the white rice. This must be previously washed with plenty of water, approximately four or five times, until the water is completely clean. Put the drained rice in a pan with water (the normal proportion is one cup of rice 160g, per 240ml of water). Leave to stand for about 30 minutes. Then cover the pan and place over a high heat. When boiled, take off the lid, lower the heat and leave to cook for around 12 minutes. Then switch off the heat and leave the rice to stand covered for about 10 minutes. To finish, stir it gently to air it, taking care not to break the grains. In a pan over a high heat, add the soy sauce, *sake*, *mirin*, ginger juice and sugar. When boiling, remove from the heat, leave to stand for one minute and then add the minced chicken. Return the pan to the heat and stir all the ingredients together until the liquid has practically evaporated. In a frying pan over a medium heat, add the eggs, tablespoon of *mirin*, and teaspoon of sugar to make the scrambled eggs. Blanch the green beans in water with a pinch of salt. Drain them and cut them diagonally. Fill two thirds of the individual bowls with white rice and separately pour the three different mixtures over the top.

Domburi is a ceramic or porcelain bowl bigger than a normal rice bowl. The recipe is named after the bowl that it is served in. A rice base covered with meat or fish that is normally served on its own.

Level of difficulty: medium
Preparation time: 50 minutes
Cooking time: 25 minutes

Gyudon
Domburi with flakes of veal

Serves 4 people
4 cups rice
500g veal
1 litre dashi *stock*
200ml soy sauce
125g sugar
200ml sake
Grated ginger
Red pepper

Prepare the white rice (see *Sanshoku soboro don*, page 54) and fill two thirds of each bowl with rice. Cut the veal into very fine strips and boil in a pan with the *dashi* stock (see *Misoshiru*, page 12), soy sauce, sugar, *sake* and grated ginger until cooked. Place the meat and grated ginger in the bowls on top of the rice.

Decorate with some strips of red pepper.

Domburi is one of the most popular recipes in Japanese cuisine and is usually served on its own. The white rice that is at the bottom of the bowl takes the flavours and aromas from the food above it.

Level of difficulty: medium
Preparation time: 50 minutes
Rice cooking time: 30 minutes

Battera
Rice with mackerel in vinegar

Serves 4 people
500g rice prepared for sushi
4 mackerel fillets
Rice vinegar
Salt

Clean the mackerel fillets and remove the skin from two of them.

Make diamond shaped incisions in the skin of the other two fillets.

Add salt and leave to stand for 30 minutes.

Clean the fillets and leave to marinate in a container full of rice vinegar for 20 minutes.

Prepare the *sushi* rice (see *Maki zushi*, page 46). When it is cold, spread the bottom of a rectangular mould (*battera*) with a layer of rice about two centimetres in thickness.

Place the two skinless fillets on top and fill the top of the mould with another layer of rice. Cover the rice with the other two mackerel fillets, with the skin facing upwards and press downwards.

Just before serving, remove from the mould and cut into portions of about two or three centimetres wide.

Battera is the name of the mould in which this recipe is made. It has a cover which allows you to press the rice together with the chosen ingredients.

Level of difficulty: medium
Preparation time: 15 minutes
Rice cooking time: 30 minutes

Onigiri
Rice triangles

Serves 4 people
400g rice prepared for sushi
2 nori *seaweed leaves*
80g umeboshi *plums*
40g dried tuna
Soy sauce
Salt

Prepare the *sushi* rice (see *Maki zushi*, page 46). Wet your hands with water so that the grains of rice do not stick to them. Also sprinkle a little salt onto your palms. Take a ball of rice in one hand and mix with the filling. The filling can be either dried tuna mixed with soy sauce or *umeboshi* plums.

Then, make a triangular shape with the mixture.

To finish, place a strip of *nori* seaweed around the triangle to help you to hold it when eating.

This is the Japanese equivalent of our sandwich. It is a typical meal for school excursions and ideal for a quick meal.

Sashimi
Assorted raw fish

Level of difficulty: medium
Preparation time: 45 minutes

Serves 4 people
160g pompano
160g tuna
160g salmon
160g white sea bass fish
160g red snapper fish

Clean the different fish chosen to make the *sashimi*. To ease the cutting, prepare the fish in 5cm strips. Just before serving, cut the fish strips with a sharp narrow bladed knife. The length can vary from a few millimetres to a centimetre.

This visibly easy dish in Japan requires a sophisticated and careful preparation as well as formal presentation at the table.

Level of difficulty: medium
Preparation time: 20 minutes
Cooking time: 1 minute

Katsuo no tataki
Tuna *tataki*

Serves 4 people
200g tuna loin
40g fish roe
50g daikon radish (also known as mooli)
2/3 garlic cloves
1 chilli
Seasonal herbs
(Shiso, turnip sprouts, spring onon, etc.)

For the *ponzu* sauce:
5ml soy sauce
5ml citric juice (yuzu, lemon, lime, etc.)

Lightly brown the sliced garlic and put to one side. Put the tuna in a frying pan and lightly fry. Remove from the heat and cool quickly in iced water so that it does not cook in the middle. When cold, cut in diagonal slices of approximately one centimetre and place on plates. It is not recommended to put the tuna in the fridge as it hardens. Grate the *daikon* (*mooli*) and place in the centre of the plate. Cover with chopped chilli and fish roe. Complement the dish with aromatic in-season herbs and baste with the *ponzu* sauce.

Typical dish from the south of Japan. It was invented when an emperor banned eating raw fish. People superficially roasted it to pretend it was cooked.

Toro to uni no sashimi
Ventresca tuna and sea urchin sashimi

Level of difficulty: medium
Preparation time: 20 minutes

Serves 4 people
200g ventresca tuna
4 sea urchins, 6-7cm in diameter
1 spring onion
4 tablespoons soy sauce
1 egg yolk
Toasted sesame
Nori *seaweed*
Wasabi

Clean the *ventresca* tuna, cut into thick strips to ease cutting and then finely slice them and put onto plates. Clean the fresh urchins, dispose of the shells and place the urchins on top of the *ventresca* slices. Mix the egg yolk with the chopped spring onion and pour a teaspoonful on each plate. Also add a tablespoon of soy sauce to the plate. Finish the plate with a *nori* seaweed decoration, a *wasabi* pyramid and a pinch of white sesame.

Ventresca must be served cold. To avoid an increase in temperature, keep it in a chilled larder. This dish is served on special occasions.

Level of difficulty: medium
Preparation time: 20 minutes
Cooking time: 2 seconds

Suzuki no carpaccio
Sea bass carpaccio

Serves 4 people

400g sea bass fillet
4 small squid (or small octopus)
8 scallops
40g shiitake mushrooms
1 spring onion, finely sliced
1 small cup soy sauce
1 small cup oil
1 tablespoon butter
Sesame seeds

Cut the sea bass into very thin slices, add salt and spread them out over a serving dish. Heat a small cupful of oil to 200°C and pour over the top of the sea bass carpaccio. Quickly place the sea bass slices onto a sheet of kitchen roll to collect the excess oil. Meanwhile, sauté the shiitake mushrooms, scallops and clean squid or small octopus in a frying pan with a little salt over a high heat. When practically cooked, lower the heat and add the soy sauce, butter and finely sliced spring onion to the frying pan. Place the sea bass slices on a plate in a fan shape and serve with the sautéed ingredients.

The dish can be decorated with toasted sesame seeds.

The oil that is poured over the sea bass at a high temperature lightly cooks the fish.

Level of difficulty: medium
Preparation time: 30 minutes
Cooking time: 2 minutes

Yaki ika mentai
Roasted squid with cod roe

Serves 4 people
200g squid
4 teaspoons cod roe
Toasted sesame seeds
Nori *seaweed*
Grated lemon rind

Clean the squid thoroughly, totally removing the membrane from the outside to avoid them from shrinking and ruffling when cooking.

Cut into pieces of 8-10 centimetres and cook either directly over the heat, in a very hot frying pan or grill without oil until they are toasted. While they are hot, make some fine decorative cuts in the fish to add texture and absorb the flavours from the other ingredients.

To finish, add a teaspoon of cod roe, a pinch of *nori* seaweed cut into strips, and grated lemon rind.

Scatter with the sesame seeds.

The most difficult part of this dish is the decorative cuts in the squid; they must be made with a very sharp knife.

Kamo no yakiniku
Duck magret with soy sauce and *mirin*

Level of difficulty: medium
Preparation time: 20 minutes
Cooking time: 5 minutes

Serves 4 people
1 duck magret
8 spring onions

For the sauce:
1 cup soy sauce
1 glass mirin
50g sugar
2 garlic cloves

Cut the duck into fine slices of about 5mm thick. Place in a very hot frying pan with very little oil for a moment and then quickly remove from the heat.

Sauté the spring onions, peel them and use to decorate the plate.

Put all the ingredients for the sauce in a pan over the heat and bring to the boil. Leave the sauce to reduce until a caramel texture is formed.

Place the frying pan with the duck over the heat again. Add the sauce and allow to cook.

This dish can be served with a bowl of white rice (see *Sanshoku soboro don*).

Level of difficulty: low
Preparation time: 20 minutes
Cooking time: 15 minutes

Buta no shogayaki
Ginger pork

Serves 4 people

400g pork fillet or loin
5cm ginger, grated
4 tablespoons soy sauce
3 small cups white rice
8 green beans

Cut the pork fillets diagonally in fine slices (if using loin of pork, cut in slices about 5cm wide and 2cm thick). Add to a bowl and leave to marinate with the four tablespoons of soy sauce and a little grated ginger, for fifteen minutes. Meanwhile, boil the rice and green beans and put to one side. Cook the pork slices in a frying pan with a little vegetable oil and heat until they are slightly brown. Serve on a bed of rice and with green beans.

This popular dish forms part of the daily Japanese diet.

World Cuisine

Desserts

Level of difficulty: medium
Preparation time: 45 minutes
Anko cooking time: 3 hours
45 minutes
Rice cooking time: 30 minutes

Sakuramochi
Rice balls wrapped
with preserved cherry leaves

Ingredients for 25 balls
*250g glutinous rice
(domivogï)
100g sugar
380ml water
25 preserved cherry leaves
Red colouring*

For the filling *(anko):*
*500g azuki beans
500g sugar
50g glucose
Salt*

Mix the water with the sugar, add colouring and rice. Leave to stand for 5 minutes. Steam over a high heat for 30 minutes. Stir the mixture with a wooden spoon until a homogeneous paste is formed.

Place in a bowl and cover with a damp cloth and aluminium foil to keep the paste hot. Leave to stand for one hour and stir again before starting to make the balls.

To make the *anko*, leave the *azuki* beans to soak for 12 hours. Change the water, boil for 45 minutes and drain. Put them in a pan over a medium heat with a little water. When it starts to boil, stir in the sugar, a pinch of salt and the glucose, little by little. A marzipan texture should form (after about three hours). Leave to cool.

Take a small amount of rice mixture and spread out over the palm of your hand. Put the filling on top and roll the mixture with your hands to make a small ball. Wrap the ball with a preserved cherry leaf.

In Japan, sweets do not exist as in England, rather they are eaten between meals and served with tea. The Japanese love the contrast between sweet and sour. *Sakuramochi* is a typical sweet eaten in the spring.

Level of difficulty: medium
Preparation time: 20 minutes
Anko cooking time: 3 hours
45 minutes
Rice cooking time: 20 minutes

Daifuku to kusamochi
Rice flour and *yomogi* herb balls

Ingredients for 20 balls
250g glutinous rice flour
300ml water
100g sugar
1 teaspoon yomogi *herb in powder*
Anko *(see page 78)*

First make the *anko* mixture. Mix the flour and water and boil in a bowl set over simmering water for 20 minutes. Remove the dough from the heat and divide into two bowls. Add half of the sugar to one of the bowls and stir with a wooden spoon until a white, compact and homogeneous dough is formed. Mix the other half of the sugar with the powdered *yomogi* herb then add to the other bowl with the dough, and stir with a wooden spoon. Sprinkle a little corn flour on the working surface and mix together the two doughs. Finally, with a rolling pin, roll out the dough until the thickness is about 5mm. Place tablespoons of *anko* (see *Sakuramochi*, page 78) over the dough, then cut into portions, seal and form small round balls.

These are very typical sweets in Japan and are most popular in spring.

Level of difficulty: medium
Preparation time: 60 minutes
Cooking time: 20 minutes

Matcha kintoki
Green tea mousse with raspberry *coulis* and *ogura*

Serves 10 people
For the green tea mousse:
250g double cream (35% fat)
125ml milk
50g egg yolk
50g sugar
10g green tea powder
500ml water
5g gelatine

For the raspberry *coulis*:
150g raspberries
50g sugar
1g gelatine leaves

For the *ogura*:
125g anko (see page 78)
125ml whipping cream

Completely dissolve the gelatine leaves in cold water. Beat the egg yolks with three-quarters of the sugar until light. Meanwhile, heat the milk in a saucepan. When it starts to simmer, remove from the heat and add the egg and sugar mixture. Place back on the heat. Increase the temperature to 85 °C. Now strain and add the dissolved gelatine. Add the powdered green tea that has been mixed with the remaining sugar (to stop lumps forming), and beat thoroughly. When it is approximately 20 °C, mix in the double cream. Pour into individual moulds.

To make the raspberry *coulis*, dissolve the gelatine in plenty of water. Now place the raspberries and the dissolved gelatine over the heat and cook until the mixture thickens. Pour into a mould and allow to cool. Cut pieces of sponge to the same size as the green tea moulds and place on top. Cover the individual servings with a layer of raspberry *coulis*. Turn out.

To make the *ogura*, mix the whipping cream and the *anko* (see *Sakuramochi*, page 78), and add to the dessert as the final layer.

It is extremely important to thoroughly mix the green tea powder and sugar before combining them with the remaining ingredients.

Sano
Mango coulis with chocolate and ginger mousse and *yokan*

Level of difficulty: high
Preparation time: 60 minutes
Cooking time: 1 hour 30 minutes

Serves 10 people
For the mango coulis:
150g mango pulp
50g sugar

For the chocolate and ginger mousse:
250g Araguani chocolate (72% cocoa)
225g cream (35% fat)
120g milk
5g fresh grated ginger
1.5g gelatine

For the *yokan*:
150ml water
150g sugar
4g agar-agar
250g white anko
5g green tea powder
50g glucose

Boil the mango pulp and sugar in a pan over a low heat for about 20 minutes (or until the required texture is formed). Empty the mixture into the bottom of a normal glass or dessert glass.

To make the chocolate and ginger mousse, first dissolve the gelatine in plenty of water. Heat the milk and grated ginger in a pan. When the milk starts to boil, cover the pan and leave to stand for 10 minutes. Sieve the mixture and add more fresh milk until it weighs 120g again. Add the gelatine to the milk and ginger, stir and pour this mixture over the chocolate. Use a blender to form a thick and creamy texture. Add the half whipped cream and pour the mousse over the top of the mango coulis. Decorate with a few dices of mango or green tea jelly.

For the green tea jelly (*yokan*), leave the agar-agar to soak for 5-6 hours and then boil until it has completely dissolved. Strain; add the glucose and sugar mixed with the green tea powder. Bring to the boil and add the white *anko* (made in the same way as *anko* with *azuki* beans but with white beans instead (see *Sakuramochi*, page 78). Leave to boil, stir continuously until thick, pour into a mould and leave to cool.

The combination of chocolate and ginger creates an original taste which is something totally different for the Western palate.

Level of difficulty: high
Preparation time: 40 minutes
Cooking time: 15 minutes

Matcha mousse
Green tea mousse

Serves 10 people
For the green tea mousse:
250g cream (35% fat)
125ml milk
50g egg yolk
50g sugar
10g green tea powder
500ml water
5g gelatine

For the *sponge*:
100g marzipan
90g egg
25g butter
30g soft flour
1g baking powder

For the raspberry coulis:
50g raspberries
1/2 gelatine leaf

To make the green tea mousse; first dissolve the gelatine in the water. Heat the milk and green tea powder, when the milk starts to boil, remove from the heat and leave to stand for 10 minutes. Sieve the mixture and add the gelatine to it. Stir. Whisk the yolks and sugar. When thick, pour the milk mixture onto it and blend well. Whip the cream and add it, then, when beginning to thicken pour two thirds into each mould (e.g. individual jelly moulds or ramekins). Leave the moulds in the fridge.

For the sponge, heat the marzipan to 50°C in a microwave and place in a large container. Add the beaten egg little by little, stirring quickly (you could use a blender). When the marzipan and egg are mixed together, reduce the speed but keep blending until a fluffy texture is formed. Slowly melt the butter in a pan over the heat. At the same time, sieve the flour and baking powder. Mix a quarter of the marzipan and egg dough with the butter, and then add the rest of the dough. To finish, add the flour and baking powder little by little, stirring continuously. Knead the dough and spread onto an oven tray. Place in the oven at 200°C for 6 minutes.

To make the raspberry coulis, dissolve the gelatine in plenty of water. Heat the raspberries and dissolved gelatine in a pan until it thickens and leave to cool in a mould. Cut a slice of sponge to the size of the bottom of the mould (containing the green tea mousse). Spread a layer of raspberry coulis over the top of the sponge. Use this as a lid for the green tea mould and turn upside down.

> The green tea in this recipe loses its sour taste and is the main ingredient in this dish.

Level of difficulty: medium
Preparation time: 20 minutes
Anko cooking time: 3 hours
45 minutes
Dough cooking time: 20 minutes

Dorayaki
Pancakes filled with *anko*

Ingredients for 15 pancakes
2 eggs
150g sugar
60g honey
3g baking soda
200g flour
150ml water
3g baking powder
Anko *(see page 78)*

First make the *anko* mixture (see page 78). Stir the eggs, sugar and honey into a bowl, then add the flour and baking soda. Gradually add the water and stir continuously until a uniformed dough is formed. *Dorayaki* is cooked in a frying pan (turning the pancakes over when bubbles start to show) and each serving consists of 2 pancakes filled with *anko*.

It is the favourite afternoon snack for Japanese children.

Authors' selection

Hiromitsu Nozaki
Waketokuyama Restaurant
(Tokyo)

Hiromitsu Nozaki was born in Fukushima in 1953. After working as a chef in the Tokyo Grand Hotel and the Happo-en, during 1980 he became head chef at the Tokuyama and Waketokuyama restaurants. He has published more than twenty cookbooks and is one of the most famous, popular and respected cooks in Japan. In his exceptional art, he combines culinary techniques with nutritional concepts. His recipes are always easy to understand.

Seiji Yamamoto
Ryugin Restaurant
(Tokyo)

After graduating from the cooking school in Tokyo, he worked for three years in several restaurants. At 22 years of age, he started working in the Aoyagi kitchen, one of the most prestigious restaurants in Tokyo, specialising in Japanese cuisine, where he worked for eleven years. On 23rd December 2003, he opened his own restaurant, the well-known Ryugin restaurant in Roppongi (Tokyo).

Hiromitsu Nozaki

Tomato to miruku no zeri
Tomato and milk jelly

Serves 4 people
1/2 kg tomatoes
550ml milk
30g flavourless jelly powder
100g sugar

Place a pan over the heat filled with 550ml of milk, and add 50g of the sugar and 15g of the powdered jelly. When the sugar and jelly powder have melted empty the milk out into a mould and leave to cool. Place the tomatoes into boiling water for a few seconds and peel them. Chop them, discard the seeds and put the remainder in a pan over the heat along with the remaining sugar and powdered jelly. When dissolved, remove from the heat and leave to cool. When the milk jelly has solidified, add the tomato jelly to the mould. When the two jellies are completely cold and have formed the appropriate texture, the dish is ready to be served.

Hiromitsu Nozaki

Renkon tofu
Lotus root *tofu*

Serves 4 people
*Lotus root (*renkon*)*
Powdered kudzu
Salty umeboshi plum paste
Green soy
Kombu *stock*
Dashi *stock (see page 12)*
Tamari
Rice vinegar

First, boil the lotus root until soft. Put the following in a pan over a high heat: five cups of *kombu* stock, two cups of powdered *kudzu* stock and two cups from the above lotus roots mixture. Stir until the mixture thickens. When it starts to consolidate, lower the heat and keep stirring the paste for fifteen minutes. Place a piece of cling film inside a cup and empty the paste into the cup. Cover the cup with another piece of cling film and hold in place using an elastic band. Submerge the cup in iced water. Separately, heat 300ml of *dashi* stock in a pan (see *Misoshiru*, page 12). Add two tablespoons of salty *umeboshi* plum paste, a tablespoon of *tamari* soy sauce and a tablespoon of rice vinegar. Add some powdered *kudzu* to thicken this sauce and leave to cool. Empty the curdled lotus root paste from the cup and place in the centre of the plates. Decorate with green soy and surround with the *umeboshi* sauce.

Hiromitsu Nozaki

Kabocha zeri
Pumpkin jelly

Serves 4 people
1 small pumpkin
Flavourless jelly powder
Sugar

For the *muscovado* syrup:
200ml water
150g muscovado sugar
130g icing sugar
1 tablespoon vinegar
2 tablespoons glucose

Peel the pumpkin, chop it and steam until soft. Drain well to remove excess water. Boil the pumpkin in a pan with water, sugar and jelly using 200ml water, 100g sugar and 5g jelly for every 300g pumpkin.

When this has dissolved, empty into a bowl or mould and leave to cool. Then cut the pumpkin jelly into 3-4cm cubes. Separately heat a litre of water with 50g of sugar and 25g of jelly powder until dissolved. Empty into a bowl and leave to cool. When this second colourless jelly starts to solidify, empty into a square mould and place a pumpkin cube in each mould. Leave to cool. To prepare the *muscovado* syrup, heat the water, the two types of sugar, the vineger and the glucose in a pan until totally melted. Place the pumpkin jelly onto the plate and pour the syrup on top.

Hiromitsu Nozaki

Ninjin to neri dofu
Carrots with *tofu* paste

Serves 4 people
Large carrots, peeled
Tofu
1 tablespoon crushed white sesame
1 tablespoon cream
1-2 teaspoons light soy sauce
Chrysanthemum petals
Judas' ear mushrooms
Sugar

For the stock:
1 litre dashi stock
5g salt
2.5ml light soy sauce
5ml sake

For the marinade:
1 litre dashi stock
10g salt
2.5ml light soy sauce
5ml sake
Dry tuna

Cut the carrots into 5cm length pieces and take out the middle to form tubes. Boil in water and then boil again but this time in a stock previously made by heating 1 litre of *dashi* stock (see *Misoshiru*, page 12) with salt, light soy sauce and *sake*.

Wrap the *tofu* in a cloth and exert pressure to remove excess water. Crush the *tofu* to obtain a purée and then add sugar, light soy sauce, crushed white sesame and cream. Stir well to mix all the ingredients together.

Boil the chrysanthemum petals, drain and finely chop them.

Blanch Judas' ear mushrooms in water and cut them in slices. Drain and submerge in the marinade. To make the marinade: Bring a litre of *dashi* stock to the boil and flavour with salt, light soy sauce and *sake*. Add the dry tuna and strain.

Drain the flower petals and mushrooms. Mix them with the already made *tofu* paste and fill in the carrot tubes. Cut the carrots in approximately 1cm pieces and place on the plate.

Shake to kabu maki
Salmon and turnip roll

Hiromitsu Nozaki

Serves 4 people
Turnip
Kelp seaweed
Smoked salmon
Celtuce lettuce
Soy leaves
Okara

Cut the smoked salmon in same sized strips as the turnip. Boil the *celtuce* lettuce until it starts to colour. Peel the turnip and leave to soak in water with salt and kelp algae for one hour. Drain the turnip and dry. Then prepare the rolls and bathe them in *okara* (soy pulp). To prepare the *okara*, put the soy leaves in a sieve and submerge in water until soft. Strain and spread out on the grill to toast them. During the cooking, add salt and vinegar.

Cut the rolls to the desired size and decoratively place them on the plates.

Seiji Yamamoto

Haru no yasai sarada
Spring salad

Serves 4 people
Bamboo roots
Udo (aralia cordata)
Bracken leaves
Petasites
Rape flower
Broad beans
Pinto beans
Ginger
Edible flowers
Dried tuna powder
Chilli
Bran rice
Happo stock (lightly seasoned stock)
Kombu stock
Dried tuna flakes
Soy sauce
Tamari
Salt

Blanch the bamboo roots in water with a pinch of bran rice and chilli. When cold, peel and boil in the *happo* stock, which is made from dried tuna flakes, soy sauce and salt.

Peel the *udo* shoots (*Aralia cordata*) and cut into very fine slices.

Blanch the bracken leaves in water with charcoal ash and then leave to soak in the stock.

Blanch the petasites, peel and add to the *happo* stock with the bracken leaves.

Also blanch the rape flower, drain and leave in the stock.

Boil the *pinto* beans that have been soaking for 12 hours, until they are soft.

Boil the broad beans for 30 minutes in a stock made up of soy sauce and salt and then strain and put to one side.

Peel the ginger and cut into tiny 1mm cubes. Prepare the dried tuna powder stock (*dashinomoto*) in a blender with some drops of fermented *tamari* soy sauce, which is stronger than a normal soy sauce. Once you have carried out the previous steps, finely chop the vegetables and decoratively display on plate. Scatter a little dried tuna powder and chopped ginger on top and finish by decorating with the chosen edible flowers.

Seiji Yamamoto

Anagojiru
Conger soup

Serves 4 people
White pumpkin
Basil seeds
700g conger
1 kombu 5 x 5cm
400ml water
Dried tuna flakes
Soy sauce
Powdered kudzu
Dashi *stock (see page 12)*
Salt
Sake

Clean and cut the white pumpkin into fine strips of 1.5cm in length. Boil in plenty of salted water. When they start to cook, strain and quickly put in cold water. Dry and submerge in *dashi* stock (see *Misoshiru*, page 12).

Dehydrate the basil seeds.

Clean the conger well and make cuts every 6cm to break the bone but without chopping the fish up. Sprinkle with a pinch of powdered *kudzu* and boil in water with a little salt. Leave the *kombu* algae to soak for two hours in plenty of water. After this time has passed, heat the water to 95°C. Just before it starts to boil, add the dried tuna flakes. Filter the stock to clean it and make it clear. Add salt, soy sauce and *sake*. Put the boiled conger, strips of pumpkin and basil seeds in a bowl and add the stock.

Seiji Yamamoto

Kaisen don
Rice with mixed seafood

Serves 4 people
Tiger prawns
Clams
Abalones
Japanese clams (rabioso)
Asian clams (Corbicula fluminea)
Sea urchins
Hornwort (Ceratophyllum demersum)
Rice
Soy sauce
Powdered kudzu
Kombu
Sake

First make the *kombu* stock, then add the *sake* to it. Boil the clams in this stock.

Vacuum-pack the abalones and boil for 12 hours.

Boil the Japanese and Asian clams in plenty of water and take out the shells.

Blanch the prawns, only half cooking them and boil the hornwort with a little salt.

Wash the rice and leave to soak in water for 15 minutes. Drain.

Add the soy sauce to the *kombu* stock and boil the rice in this stock over a low heat. When boiling, lower the heat. After five minutes, lower the heat again and leave the rice for ten minutes before taking off the heat. Leave to rest for another 10-15 minutes. Drain and keep the stock to one side. Chop all the ingredients up and place over the boiled rice. Place the sea urchins on top of these ingredients.

Mix the powdered *kudzu* with the *kombu* stock and place over a low heat. When it thickens, pour over the rice and the rest of the ingredients.

Decorate the plate with hornwort.

Unagi no kabayaki
Roasted eel with sweetened thick soy sauce

Seiji Yamamoto

Serves 4 people
Eel
Wasabi
Sanshou *pepper*
Iwanashi *herb (Epigaea asiatica)*

For the *teriyaki* sauce:
Soy sauce
Sugar candy
Tamari *(thick soy sauce)*
Mirin
Sake
Honey
Dissolved sugar

Clean the eel and cut off the head to remove all of the blood. Gut the eel and remove the bones and fins. Using a knife, make small incisions along the skin of the eel to remove unnecessary fat.

The *teriyaki* sauce is made by mixing and heating all of the ingredients in a saucepan until the sugar is completely dissolved. Roast the eel on a grill and baste in the *teriyaki* sauce a couple of times while cooking.

When it is cooked, cut into 5cm length pieces and place on the plate.

Serve with grated *wasabi*, Japanese *sanshou* pepper and *iwanashi* herbs.

Drinks

Rice is also the basic element of the most emblematic Japanese drink: *sake,* of which there are hundreds of varieties. Some of the traditional drinks are *shochu,* a distillation similar to vodka; *umeshu,* a smooth plum liquor; and *awamori,* distilled from rice. However, the most popular is beer; the Japanese give a toast with this on a daily basis, "Kampai" (cheers).

Legends state that ancient gods made *sake* from the first rice that was grown in each New Year. Other stories say that *sake* is able to fight away the spirits. Legends aside, it is certain that *sake* appeared around the 2nd century BC, when rice was introduced to Japan along with new plantation techniques.

For centuries, it was made only to be consumed in the imperial palace or in the event of rites and celebrations. It was considered a sacred drink. However, in the 17th century, its status changed. They started to produce it by the current methods and it became available to the general public.

Sake, the drink of the gods

Sake is a transparent and colourless drink, with between 14% and 16% of alcohol. Its production process is similar to that of beer, as both use cereals that are capable of producing sugar, which is converted into alcohol. However, *sake* is not carbonated; it also keeps a wide range of aromas and flavours that resembles some of the best wines. Two basic elements are needed to make *sake:* rice and water. The rice, the *sakamai* type, is not the same rice that is used for cooking. It is a whiter and more opaque cereal, with less dense starch in the centre of the grain. The quality of water is also important. In the past, water was used from the rivers or lakes. Currently, well-filtered underground water is used. The Japanese regions with the best rice and water, found in the north of the country, are also

those that produce the best *sake*. Cold temperatures are also required; therefore, it is produced in winter and in the northern regions.

Its complicated production process starts by extracting the golden husk from the rice and scraping off the grain until arriving at the centre. Then, the rice is washed with water, left to soak for a while, cooked and left to cool. One part of this rice goes to make *koji,* malt-rice, from where the necessary enzyme is extracted to obtain sugar. The initial rice, *koji* and baking powder undergo several mixtures so that the *koji* transforms the starch from the rice into sugar and the baking powder ferments

the alcohol. The obtained substance is filtered, left to stand to separate the sediment and heated at 60 degrees to eliminate bacteria. After another rest period in tanks, the *sake* is bottled.

Traditionally, *sake* was made only with rice, but during the Second World War, some factories started to add alcohol in order to avoid a shortfall in rice production in the country, due to the conflicts. From then on, two types of *sake* were produced: one made only from rice and another made with additives. Additionally, each one of these groups is subdivided into other *sake* varieties, according to the grade of the rice before fermentation.

The rigid Japanese laws established a new classification, according to the quality of *sake* (superior, first class or second class). Apart from the differing production methods and the classes established by the law, the consumer is also able to distinguish between the sweet and dry varieties, according to the levels of sugar and souring additives. The variety with the highest quality is *ginjoshu,* although it is hard to get because it is only home produced. The most popular *sake,* and the one that is exported the most has a sweet aroma and mild taste. There are many types of *sake,* therefore many different ways to drink it. Generally, it is drunk cold or at room temperature, although some stronger ones are heated at 40 degrees and drunk lukewarm. The Japanese serve it in small glasses as well as ceramic ones, which are decorated with traditional art motives.

Generally, *sake* is best served with light dishes, such as fish, chicken or pasta, although it is usually drunk on its own.

Shochu, Southern distillation

Another of Japan's indigenous drinks is the *shochu,* distilled in a similar fashion to *vodka* and an alcohol percentage of between 25% and 40%. Unlike the *sake,* which requires cold temperatures for its correct fermentation, this is made in hotter areas, mainly in the south of the country: the west part of the main island, Honshu and Kyushu Island.

Shochu is the result of a distillation with various ingredients, such as rice, sweet potatoes, wheat, barley and cane sugar. The strongest variety is made from potatoes, whilst the mildest is made from rice. Depending on the distillation method, there are two types of *shochu*: *Honkaku*, produced with a single distillation, keeping the essence of its ingredients, and *Korui*, made from several distillation processes, which produces a milder liquor. Its distillation process has been compared to that of the best Scottish whiskies. The Japanese drink *shochu* on its own or with hot water, a combination known as *oyu-wari*. In the last few decades, *shochu* has also gained popularity amongst younger people who drink it with soft drinks or tea.

Awamori, rice distillation

Awamori is made in the small Okinawa islands, which are in the south of the country and have a tropical climate. Once again, rice is the base of this liquor. It is different from *sake* because it undergoes a distillation process. It originates from Thailand and is a good example of the cultural exchanges between Eastern countries, as it is also made in Taiwan, China and Korea. One of the differences between *awamori* and other indigenous drinks from Japan such as *sake* or *shochu*, is that a longer type of rice that comes from Thailand is used for its production. In addition, *awamori* increases in quality over the years. It is said to reach its prime 25 years after production. The hot climate in the Okinawa islands makes the liquor unique, with citric flavours and an alcohol percentage of between 25% and 30%.

Umeshu, a revitalising liquor

Owing to its relaxing and revitalising effects, *umeshu* is also a liquor that is often found in Japanese homes. It is made from the country's plums, characterised by its acidic flavours and high content of potassium and iron. Its popularity is also due to its mild aroma and a balanced combination of bitterness and sweetness. In Japanese literature, you can find numerous references to the effects of this heralded recipe, such as, elimination of fatigue, helping the body to recuperate energy and vitality, reducing hunger pangs and cleaning the digestive system.

Beer, the most popular drink

While *sake* seems to be the most well known Japanese drink around the world, in actual fact the most popular drink in the bars is beer. It was first introduced to the country in the middle of the 19th century. The first manufacturing beer factories were in Hokkaido island and in the outskirts of Tokyo, although in the last few decades small sized factories have appeared, which has increased the beer supply to the local market. The most popular factories are Asahi, Kirin, Suntory and Sapporo, which produce lager and dark beers, as well as a mixture of both varieties.

Index

World Cuisine Morocco

With dishes by:
Mohamed Fedal • Frederic Petreau • Fatema Hal

World Cuisine Italy (II)

With d...
Antone...

World Cuisine Italy (I)

With dishes by:
Antonello Colonna • Carlo Cracco

*Vitello impanato alla milanese
con petali di pomodoro gratinati*
Breaded Milanese veal with tomato

Carlo Cracco

Serves 4
1kg veal
3 eggs
200g fresh white breadcrumbs
200g butter
12 tomatoes, skinned, halved,
deseeded
200g spinach
200g butter
100g finely chopped mixed
herbs
Culture, parsley, tarragon)
Maldon salt

First, clean the steak, removing any fat or sinews. Cut into
four 4.5cm pieces.

Next, coat the pieces in the egg and breadcrumbs, and fry
in butter until golden, but pink inside. Take off the heat and
leave for two or three minutes. Place in a pre-heated 200°C
oven and bake for two to three minutes. Season with Maldon
salt and pepper.

Meanwhile, melt the butter and mix with the breadcrumbs
and herbs. Season. Spread the mixture between two sheets
of greaseproof paper and leave to cool in the fridge for two
hours. Take out and cut into small, circular disks using a
pastry cutter. Fry lightly on both sides until golden.

Sauté the spinach with a little oil and spoon into the
tomatoes. Assemble on top of the bread disk and use to
garnish.

Authors' selection | 58

The Times World Cook Book Collection Offer (120 Page Full Colour volumes)

Title	Available for purchase from:	Price (inc P&P)	Quantity	Total (£)
Italy I (60pp Sampler)	29-Oct-2005	£1.99		
Italy II	05-Nov 2005	£3.98		
Morocco	12-Nov 2005	£3.98		
USA	19-Nov 2005	£3.98		
India I	26-Nov 2005	£3.98		
India II	03-Dec 2005	£3.98		
Japan	10-Dec 2005	£3.98		
South America	17-Dec 2005	£3.98		
Scandinavia	24-Dec 2005	£3.98		
Portugal	31-Dec 2006	£3.98		
Thailand I	07-Jan 2006	£3.98		
Thailand II	14-Jan 2006	£3.98		
Greece	21-Jan 2006	£3.98		
France I	28-Jan 2006	£3.98		
France II	04-Feb 2006	£3.98		
UK	11-Feb 2006	£3.98		
China	18-Feb 2006	£3.98		
Caribbean	25-Feb 2006	£3.98		
Mexico	04-Mar 2006	£3.98		
Spain	11-Mar 2006	£3.98		
Full Set *	(20% discount)	£59.99		
		Total Price		**£**

* Readers who subscribe to the Full Set will be sent a book each week until the collection is complete.
Please send 10 mastheads of any The Times or Sunday Times with each Full Set ordered.

Title: _____ Initial: _____ Surname: _____

Address: _____

_____

Postcode: _____ DOB: _____ / _____ / _____

Phone # : _____ Email: _____ @ _____

I enclose a cheque/PO made payable to 'Times Cookery Books Offer', and a newspaper
masthead (Times logo) for each book I've ordered. Price above includes postage and packing.
Send to "Times Cookery Books Offer", PO Box 142, Horsham RH13 5FJ. Please allow 28 days for delivery.

For the sum of **£**...............

Or please debit my Visa / Mastercard / Maestro for **£**..............

Card Number _____

Issue date (maestro only) ...... /.........

Start Date .... /................ Close Date.............../...............

Signature _____

Times Newspapers and ESP Promotions Ltd may directly or via
their agents, mail you about new products or services.
Tick if you don't want to receive these from Times Newspapers Limited ☐
or carefully selected companies ☐ (see our privacy policy at www.nidp.com)
ESP Promotions Ltd may contact you by post about new promotions, products and services.
If you do not want to receive these from ESP Promotions ltd tick here ☐